Invasive Plant Species Early Detection in the San Francisco Bay Area Network
2007 Annual Report

Natural Resource Report NPS/PWR/SFAN/NRTR—2008/135

Andrea Williams and Elizabeth Speith
National Park Service
San Francisco Bay Area Network
Fort Cronkhite Building 1063
San Francisco, CA 94965

July 2008

U.S. Department of the Interior
National Park Service
Natural Resource Program Center
Fort Collins, Colorado

The Natural Resource Publication series addresses natural resource topics that are of interest and applicability to a broad readership in the National Park Service and to others in the management of natural resources, including the scientific community, the public, and the NPS conservation and environmental constituencies. Manuscripts are peer-reviewed to ensure that the information is scientifically credible, technically accurate, appropriately written for the intended audience, and is designed and published in a professional manner.

The Natural Resources Technical Reports series is used to disseminate the peer-reviewed results of scientific studies in the physical, biological, and social sciences for both the advancement of science and the achievement of the National Park Service's mission. The reports provide contributors with a forum for displaying comprehensive data that are often deleted from journals because of page limitations. Current examples of such reports include the results of research that addresses natural resource management issues; natural resource inventory and monitoring activities; resource assessment reports; scientific literature reviews; and peer reviewed proceedings of technical workshops, conferences, or symposia.

Views, statements, findings, conclusions, recommendations and data in this report are solely those of the author(s) and do not necessarily reflect views and policies of the U.S. Department of the Interior, NPS. Mention of trade names or commercial products does not constitute endorsement or recommendation for use by the National Park Service.

Printed copies of reports in these series may be produced in a limited quantity and they are only available as long as the supply lasts. This report is also available from the San Francisco Area I&M Network website (http://www.nature.nps.gov/im/units/SFAN) or the Natural Resource Publications Management website (http://www.nature.nps.gov/publications/NRPM) on the internet, or by sending a request to the address on the back cover.

Please cite this publication as:

Williams, A. E. and E. Speith. 2008. Invasive plant species early detection in the San Francisco Bay Area Network: 2007 annual report. Natural Resource Technical Report NPS/PWR/SFAN/NRTR—2008/135. National Park Service, Fort Collins, Colorado.

NPS D-44, November 2008

Contents

Contents (continued

Figures

Tables

Appendixes

Executive Summary

Parks need to know where incipient populations of highly invasive plants are becoming established, and protect the most critical areas from invasion. This year was the first full field season of testing the early detection protocol. The methods detailed in this report focus on surveying road- and trail-side in priority areas using volunteers, and is based on the SFAN I&M Network's Early Detection Monitoring of Invasive Plant Species in the San Francisco Bay Area Network: A Volunteer-Based Approach (Williams et al. 2008 in review).

The Golden Gate National Recreation Area (GOGA) contains 38 subwatersheds deemed at high risk of invasion and/or harm to significant biological resources, of which 33 subwatershed were within the boundaries actively managed by the park. Searches were conducted by teams of two or three along the prioritized trails and roads in these subwatersheds looking for up to 83 plant species ranked as having the greatest risk for invasion in these areas. One thousand and one high-priority plant populations were mapped in the park. Of 66 subwatersheds searched, 45 were found to contain the highest priority species. Twenty-eight of these subwatersheds were deemed at high risk for invasion. Maps were created of all areas surveyed in the GOGA and priority plant species found. Based on results, the species list was modified to better reflect actual population levels within the park.

Volunteers played a pivotal role in the implementation of the field surveys. Fifteen volunteers over two years were worked with on a one-on-one basis to conduct surveys, contributing 543 hours, worth $9795.72. Web pages were created to educate the public about the project and provide support to existing volunteers. Collaborative efforts with staff at GOGA and the Golden Gate National Parks Conservancy were established to facilitate communication of findings and to broaden the early detection network.

Acknowledgements

In addition to the primary authors, many contributors provided critical assistance: Maria Alvarez and the Habitat Restoration Team for testing the techniques, Sharon Farrell and the Golden Gate National Parks Conservancy for support and partnership, the Sonoma Ecology Center for technical assistance and development of the GeoWeed data management system, and Jim Dougherty for endless volunteer hours and weed identification skills.

1.0 Introduction

1.1 Background

Invasive plant species negatively affect park resources and visitor enjoyment in several ways, including altering landscapes and fire regimes, reducing native plant and animal habitat, and blocking views and increasing trail maintenance needs. Invasive species are second only to habitat loss as threats to global biodiversity (e.g., Scott and Wilcove 1998). Given the extraordinary biodiversity of the San Francisco Bay Area, and the development pressure on private lands in the area, SFAN parks serve as crucial refugia for native species. Over 100 rare plant species can be found in SFAN parks. Invasive plants threaten many of these rare species: in Golden Gate National Recreation Area (GOGA) alone, 25 species of non-native plants were noted as directly threatening rare plant populations (GOGA 2004). Trails, roads and waterways are the main routes of infestations in most natural areas, and the SFAN is no exception. Monitoring the likely routes of invasion and uninfested areas is the most effective way to prevent the spread of existing species and the infestation of new species in SFAN parks (e.g., McNeely et al. 2001).

Inventory and Monitoring staff ranked both species and areas to prioritize search efforts for early detection (Williams et al. 2008, in review). The GOGA management area is divided into 29 watersheds and 149 subwatersheds (smaller subunits of watersheds based largely on drainages), based on geographical features. These subwatersheds were prioritized based on a ranking matrix containing information from three general areas: management priority for protection of rare plants and/or animals; risk of invasion due to infrastructure or habitat vulnerability; and current level of infestation. This ranking process assigned each subwatershed in the park with a high, significant, moderate, or low priority for survey (see Appendix A).

The GOGA exotic plant list, which numbers over 300 species, was also ranked to prioritize search efforts. All species were first ranked based on their status on existing lists of known invasives (California Invasive Plant Council, The Nature Conservancy, and California Food and Agriculture), and on any published literature or expert opinion which documents the plants as an ecosystem alterer or rare plant endangerer. All plants which were found to have documented invasive characteristics based on this ranking were then categorized based on biological ease of control independent of acres already infested, and feasibility of control based on existing infestation acreage and cost for removal. This process resulted in a SFAN Invasive species list of 166 plant species, half of which were in the top three lists of priority for early detection (see Appendix B). List 1 species are highly invasive but not widespread; List 2 species are highly invasive but more widespread, or moderately invasive and not widespread; List 3 species are highly invasive and widespread; List 4 species are of low to moderate invasiveness.

> ## *Looking for the worst plants in the best places*

Parks need to know where incipient populations of highly invasive plants are becoming established, and protect the most critical areas from invasion. Budget constraints necessitate looking in areas where it will do the most good—in high-quality and high-risk areas—along a primary vector for invasive plants, using volunteer labor. While surveyors may readily spot some species of weeds far from the trail in the open scrub and grasslands of SFAN parks, it is difficult to determine with high confidence where plants do not occur, particularly with species that are inconspicuous or senescent during a portion of the year or low in stature, more than a few meters from roads and trails. However, absence directly adjacent to survey corridors is still valuable to park managers as these are the most likely sites for incipient populations to become established in a park.

1.2 Objectives

Objectives for the 2007 field season were based on those from the main protocol.

1. Within GOGA, identify and inventory all roads and trails in high-priority subwatersheds, and half the significant-priority subwatersheds, noting presence and absence of priority weed species. Use visual assessment and GPS technology to detect and accurately map incipient populations of the top-priority plant species on the GOGA Invasive Plant list.

2. Train volunteers to conduct early detection surveys for top-priority SFAN Invasive Plants in the high-priority areas.

3. Train GOGA staff and park-partner staff to identify top-priority SFAN Invasive Plants for opportunistic early detection of new populations during regular work activities.

4. Revise priority species list based on information acquired during the 2007 field season.

2.0 Methods

All methodology is based on the SFAN I&M Network's Early Detection Monitoring of Invasive Plant Species in the San Francisco Bay Area Network: A Volunteer-Based Approach (Williams et al. 2008, in review). This program can be adapted to different person-hours and skill levels, allowing parks to maximize their effectiveness based on resources available. Engaging people in detection; giving them clear direction and a point person to answer questions and receive invasives reports; and following up with feedback on reports are essential components to a good program. The following section describes sampling methods, scheduling, data management and data collection.

2.1 Prioritization

Full prioritization methods can be found in the protocol, but are summarized briefly here.

2.1.1 Species

The list of target species for GOGA was based on current knowledge and rankings, summing recognized invasiveness and biological ease of control and stratifying into priorities by feasibility of control based on categories of actual or estimated species' infested acreage in the park. A list of all exotic species known or thought to occur in the park (~300 species), compiled from NPSpecies, was the base list. After removing known non-invasive species, and species locally non-native, 174 species remained. Species listed by the California Invasive Plant Council (Cal-IPC), California Department of Food and Agriculture (CDFA), The Nature Conservancy (TNC), and local Weed Management Areas received varying numbers of points for invasiveness, as did unlisted species which shared invasive characteristics with a listed congener. Based on best available knowledge, species also received points for altering ecosystems—affecting a system change, not just crowding out other plants—and for endangering rare plants in SFAN parks. Next, based on best available knowledge, species were ranked by ease of control independent of number of acres infested. All points were summed for the overall invasiveness score, then sorted according to feasibility of control based on number of acres infested with that species, cost for removal, politics, and access. Species shown to be highly invasive, but not widespread in the park, were top priority for detailed mapping; more widespread but still invasive species were mapped with a point unless populations are small.

2.1.2 Areas

The list of priority areas for searches was made by ranking subwatersheds—drainage-based subunits of watersheds—by number and degree of current infestations; risk of further infestation; and priority of resources present. Higher scores were received for low current infestation levels, high risk of further infestation based on presence of infrastructure or invadable vegetation type, and presence of rare plants or animals. Subwatersheds were ranked, grouped along the most natural breaks, and assigned a score. Total score was obtained by adding risk to weighted (2x) rare species priority score and subwatersheds approximately quartered into high, significant, moderate, and low priority. High-priority subwatersheds are visited annually; significant and moderate, biennially; and low, once every five years.

2.2 Search Areas

GOGA is divided into 29 watersheds and 149 subwatersheds, based on topography (see maps, Appendix A). Thirty-eight of these subwatersheds were deemed at high risk of invasion and/or harm to significant biological resources, of which 33 subwatersheds were within the boundaries actively managed by the park. Within these 33 subwatersheds are 69 miles of trails and roads officially mapped by GOGA staff. These roads and trails within the high-priority areas of the park were the first areas to be searched.

Maps have been made for the areas that need revisits and continued stewardship, and can be found on the inpgogamahe1:\Divisions\Network I&M\Shared\Vegetation\Invasive Plants\weedwatchers\Edsitemaps\surveyareas, as well as in Appendix C. These maps are made available for staff and the volunteer stewards who will adopt an area to patrol for new invasions.

2.3 Field Methods

Searches were conducted by teams of one to three individuals along the 69 miles of trails and roads in the high-priority areas of the park and usually covered no more than two to five miles of the project area per team per day, depending on target invasive plant densities, vegetation, and terrain. Each survey route was recorded both on a paper map of the area and digitized from a tracklog into a polyline layer using ESRI's ArcPad or ArcMap program. Though survey areas were only limited by the visual range of the surveyor, the official search area used for logging both positive (plant occurrence) and negative data (areas where target plants were not found) was restricted to a few meters on either side of the route.

Along the survey route observers recorded location and associated biological information (phenology, habitat, distribution) for all high-priority target plant populations encountered. Depending on their level of training, surveyors walked the routes looking for either the 23 highest-ranked target plant species (List 1 plants), the 52 highest-ranking plants (List 1 and 2 plants), or the 83 highest-ranking plants (List 1, 2, and 3 plants).

The level of detail of data collection was dictated by the ranking of the plant on the priority list, and the extent of the infestation. This tiered approach to data collection reduces the time needed to collect standardized, detailed data in areas of high infestations as well as the amount of training needed for beginner surveyors (Figure 1).

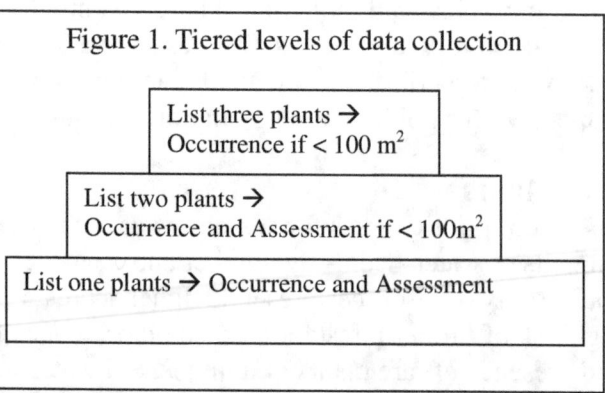

Figure 1. Tiered levels of data collection

List three plants → Occurrence if < 100 m^2

List two plants → Occurrence and Assessment if < 100m^2

List one plants → Occurrence and Assessment

For the initial survey of a route, point *occurrences* and polygon *assessments* were mapped for List 1 species; point *occurrences* and polygon *assessments* (if patch size is less than 100 m^2) for List 2 species; presence/absence, or point *occurrences* (if patch size is less than 100 m^2) for List

3 species; presence/absence recorded for lower-priority species, along with the *survey area*. For subsequent surveys most *occurrences* should already exist.

All data was collected on paper data sheets and then entered into the GOGA GeoWeed database and/or was captured in the field using hand-held GPS/PDA units installed with ESRI's Arc Pad software with the GeoWeed tool bar and then downloaded into the GeoWeed database. Downloaded and entered data were checked against field data sheets for correctness and completeness. Staff and long-term interns performed downloading and data-checking tasks.

Every mapping session (day/team) also include a new *survey area* to record absence data for species not seen, and may include an inventory of all species seen if the observer is sufficiently advanced. Assessments also include ancillary data on habitat, phenology and distribution. Species identifications for occurrences and surveys have an associated confidence level to flag potential misidentifications.

A detailed description of all field methodology can also be found the Early Detection of Invasive Plants SOP 2: Mapping and SOP 3: Field Data Collection (Williams et al. 2008, in review).

2.4 Trainings

A key element of the Weed Watcher program is engaging a maximum number of searchers in opportunistic sampling, both in incidental or passive searches, as well as directed active searching. Participants must be trained to identify target species, then to communicate location, distribution, and biological attributes to the correct entities to ensure timely response. To this end, several types of trainings were held including weed identification, invasive plant mapping, and GeoWeed database trainings. Each of these courses catered to training participants to gather increasingly detailed levels of data about weed infestations.

The "WeedID" class defined the invasive species concept, how invasive species are moved around the park and how natural resources are affected, target invasive plant identification; and how to report target plant sighting. The class was conducted through two hours of classroom instruction and one hour of field instruction. Classroom instruction relied on PowerPoint presentations, "Plant-out-of-Place" identification cards, and target species specimens whenever possible. Power Point presentations can be found at inpgogamahe1:\Divisions\Network I&M\Shared\Vegetation\Invasive Plants\weedwatchers \training\plantid_train. The "Plant-out-of-Place" cards can be found at: inpgogamahe1:\Divisions\Network I&M\Shared\Vegetation\Invasive Plants\Species\ID cards.

The invasive plant mapping course is a three-to four-hour introduction to GOGA protocols for data collection, minimum data elements needed when mapping plants, aerial and topographic map interpretation, how to mark infestations on a map, how to calibrate distance and cover estimations, introductory GPS and ESRI Arc Pad methods. This course is designed to be conducted half in classroom and half with hands-on activities outside. An optional introduction to the ArcPad GeoWeed applet can be included in an afternoon session. The PowerPoint presentation can be found at inpgogamahe1:\Divisions\Network I&M\Shared\Vegetation \Invasive Plants\weedwatchers\training\plantid_train.

Additionally, a GeoWeed database training was held to introduce data managers at GOGA to the new invasive plant data management system. The GeoWeed data management system was used to record all of the Weed Watcher data, as well as act as a conduit for this information to be transmitted to all invasive plant managers in the parks. As such, it is integral to the project's success to train as many individuals as possible at the parks to use effectively use this database. The all-day training covered the database schema, form navigation, data entry, an introduction to the GeoWeed Arc Pad applet, and GPS trouble-shooting.

2.5 Analyses/GIS Manipulations

Data from GeoWeed were examined for trends in occurrences by species type and location. Using the "filter" function, the number of occurrences for a species; total acreage for List 1 species; number of subwatersheds in which a species occurred; number of search hours and observer were also extracted. Shapefile attribute tables were examined for number of invasive species occurrences by list and subwatershed priority.

2.6 Species List Revisions

This year represented the first full field season of data collection, and the opportunity to revise the priority lists based on more objective criteria for how widespread species are in the park. The number of occurrences, and number of subwatersheds in which species were found, were examined and compared to listing level for appropriateness. Species found in more than 15 subwatersheds—10% of all park subwatersheds—were deemed too widespread for List 1, and species with over 50 occurrences were moved to List 3. List 1 species with no occurrences were thought too rare to be reliably identified by volunteers, and were moved to List 3.1: this list is for advanced observers, such as trained staff and botanists, but species are treated as List 1 for data collection purposes.

3.0 Results

Setting desired thresholds for invasive species early detection can be an odd exercise, for the greatest success—not finding plants that are not there—is the most difficult to measure. Given that, the number of miles of trails and subwatersheds covered; the number of persons trained and actively detecting, and hours spent searching; and the number of species of each priority type in each priority level subwatershed are presented below. Additionally, since this was the first full year of searching, revisions to the species list were made based on more accurate distribution data. Maps from surveys may be found in Appendix C.

3.1 Search Effort

Twenty-four miles were surveyed during the 2006 field season, and 38 during the 2007 field season, resulting in 62 total miles covered. In total, 20 individuals combined for just under 700 hours to complete these surveys; 543 of these hours were volunteer hours.

During the 2006-2007 field seasons, 45 subwatersheds were found to contain List 1 species. Twenty-eight of these subwatersheds were high-priority subwatersheds, 10 were significant-priority subwatersheds, five were moderate-priority subwatersheds, one was low priority, and one was in GOGA legislative boundaries, but not within the management boundaries of the park. Forty-two subwatersheds were found to contain List 2 target species. Twenty-five of these subwatersheds were high-priority areas, eight were significant-priority subwatersheds, five were moderate-priority areas, two were low-priority areas, and two were within GOGA legislative boundaries, but not within the management boundaries of the park. Fifty-five subwatersheds total were surveyed in 2007, while 21 subwatersheds were visited in 2006. Several of the sites visited in 2006 were revisited in 2007; 66 subwatersheds in all were visited at least once during this period. Generally, the inclusion of lower-priority subwatersheds was made based on travel routes: the less-than-high-priority subwatersheds were on the route to or from a high-priority subwatershed.

3.2 Species Found

One thousand and one individual occurrences of target weed species were mapped and entered into the GeoWeed database. Nine hundred and forty-seven of these occurrences were List 1, 2, or 3 species. Two hundred and eighty-two of these occurrences were List 1 species, 540 were List 2 species, and 125 of these occurrences were List 3 species.

Forty-two species were found during the surveys. Fourteen of the 23 List 1 species were found, 22 List 2 species, and 11 List 3 species. The lesser number of List 3 species observances is not due to lesser numbers or distribution of these species, but rather because occurrences were only recorded for plants with a patch size of less than 100 square meters, and not all surveys completed were for the entire set of List 1, 2, and 3 species. Many of the surveys with volunteer assistance as well training surveys were conducted using abbreviated plant lists, to facilitate the collection of high-quality data from individuals with less technical plant mapping experience and/or botanical identification skills.

Table 1 displays all of the List 1, 2, and 3 species, as well as the number of occurrences, found during the surveys. It should be noted that the numbers of occurrences found for each species may not be a true indication of abundance, as the delineation of individual patches is somewhat subjective for many species. For example, poison hemlock (*Conium maculatum*) can occur across the landscape at low densities (<30% cover) and still be considered a patch, thus creating many large patches of greater than 100 m^2 which are not recorded. Other species, such as jubata grass (*Cortaderia jubata*), can be delineated at a much finer scale, sometimes with individual plants comprising a single patch, resulting in more occurrences. Additionally, detectability can vary during the field season for many species (e.g. oxeye daisy (*Leucanthemum vulgare*) is not obvious from any distance except during its flowering period, whereas Monterey pine (*Pinus radiata*) is obvious year round.)

Development of the GeoWeed data management system during the 2006-2007 field season led to some data inconsistencies with the assessments of weed populations—loss of polygons, or cover class alterations/midpoint errors, for the most part, but also some misapplication of data-gathering rules (not taking a polygon for high-ranking species). These assessments include the extent and coverage of all weed populations detected and are critically important to assessing the rapid response potential and any change over time of detected populations; this information on patch size is not presented here. It should be noted that all List 1 and 2 populations recorded cover areas (assessments) of less than 100 m^2, though the cover density can vary widely. Occurrence information alone *can* be sufficient to discern new populations that require rapid response, but a true measure of success for the parks—the reduction in extent of an invasive species—will require amended assessments of weed occurrences or other monitoring of control efforts done by park staff.

3.3 Species List Revisions

Analysis of search results showed some species considered rare within the park were actually much more widespread than expert opinion ("Feasibility of Control") suggested, while others were not found. Also, learning and searching for 23 species proved to be difficult for most volunteers—especially species never found, as search images were not reinforced through an actual detection. Little confidence can be placed in absence data for such species over the long term. Therefore, species rated high but not found were transferred to "List 3.1" for staff and advanced observers: these species are treated as List 1 for data collection purposes, but volunteers are not taught to detect them until later in training. Also, results from the 2007 field season were used to shift species from Lists 1 and 2, ensuring search and data collection time will be allocated to the true "early detection" species. Some species were shifted to List 5 (dune and aquatic) for directed searches, and other lists tightened based on "total score" criteria (a measure of recognized invasiveness used in the original ranking).

Seven species found in more than 15 subwatersheds and with over 30 occurrences were shifted to List 3. One species had occurrences in 16 subwatersheds, but only 26 total occurrences, and was shifted from List 1 to List 2. Fifteen List 1 species had no occurrences; 13 were shifted to List 3.1, and two to List 5. Four List 2 species with few occurrences (found in less than five subwatersheds) were elevated to List 1; licorice plant (*Helichrysum petiolare*) was also elevated from List 2 to 1, even though its 10 occurrences were in six subwatersheds, due to its rapid spread rate and small occurrence size (most consisting of only one plant)—as well as its high priority for management in the park.

Table 1. Number of occurrences and species list revisions for GOGA based largely on 2006-2007 field results. Percentages based on 66 subwatersheds searched. Changes in **bold.**

Scientific Name	Common Name	06-07 Feas-ability of Control	Invasive-ness Score	06-07 list	06-07 #occ	06-07 #suwa	% suwa found in	08 list
Ailanthus altissima	tree-of-heaven	H	8	1	0	0	0.0%	3.1
Arctotheca calendula	capeweed	H	8	1	10	4	6.1%	1
Arundo donax	giant reed	H	9	1	2	2	3.0%	5
Carduus acanthoides	plumeless thistle		6.75	1	0	0	0.0%	3.1
Carthamus lanatus	woolly distaff thistle		7	1	0	0	0.0%	3.1
Centaurea calcitrapa	purple starthistle	H	8	1	2	1	1.5%	1
Centaurea solstitialis	yellow starthistle	H	11	1	0	0	0.0%	3.1
Cirsium arvense	Canada thistle	H	9.75	1	0	0	0.0%	3.1
Cortaderia jubata	Andean or purple pampas grass, jubata grass	H	9	1	124	22	33.3%	3
Cortaderia selloana	Uruguayan pampas grass	H	8	1	1	1	1.5%	1
Cotoneaster pannosus	silverleaf cotoneaster	H	4	1	36	15	22.7%	3
Cynodon dactylon	Bermudagrass	H	7	1	8	4	6.1%	3.1
Cytisus striatus	Portugese broom, striated broom	H	6	1	5	4	6.1%	1
Digitalis purpurea	purple foxglove	H	4	1	1	1	1.5%	1
Dittrichia graveolens	stinkweed	H	5	1	0	0	0.0%	3.1
Ehrharta calycina	perennial veldt grass	H	8	1	0	0	0.0%	3.1
Ehrharta erecta	panic veldt grass	H	7	1	56	16	24.2%	3
Hypericum perforatum	Klamathweed	H	5	1	0	0	0.0%	3.1
Mentha pulegium	pennyroyal	H	5	1	7	6	9.1%	2
Rubus discolor [*procerus*]	Himalayan blackberry	H	9	1	26	16	24.2%	2
Spartium junceum	Spanish broom	H	7	1	0	0	0.0%	3.1
Ulex europaea	gorse, furze	H	9	1	3	3	4.5%	1
Vinca major	periwinkle	H	8	1	3	2	3.0%	1
Acacia melanoxylon	blackwood acacia	M	7	2	9	5	7.6%	2
Ageratina adenophora	thoroughwort, crofton weed	L	6	2	16	6	9.1%	2
Carduus tenuiflorus	slender-flowered thistle		4.75	2	0	0		4
Carpobrotus chilensis	sea fig		5	2	0	0	0.0%	5
Carpobrotus edulis	hottentot fig, freeway iceplant	L	8	2	66	11	16.7%	3
Centaurea melitensis	Napa thistle, tocalote	L	6	2	3	2	3.0%	1
Conium maculatum	poison hemlock	L	7	2	27	13	19.7%	2
Cynara cardunculus	artichoke thistle, cardoon		5	2	0	0	0.0%	3.1
Cytisus scoparius	Scotch broom	M	9	2	17	4	6.1%	1
Delairea odorata	cape ivy	L	6.75	2	33	12	18.2%	2

9

Table 1. Number of occurrences and species list revisions for GOGA based largely on 2006-2007 field results. Percentages based on 66 subwatersheds searched. Changes in **bold**. (continued).

Scientific Name	Common Name	06-07 Feas-ability of Control	Invasive-ness Score	06-07 list	06-07 #occ	06-07 #suwa	% suwa found in	08 list
Dipsacus fullonum	common teasel, Fuller's teasel	L	5	2	8	8	12.1%	2
Eucalyptus globulus	bluegum eucalyptus	L	8.75	2	22	12	18.2%	2
Euphorbia oblongata	eggleaf or oblong spurge	M	5	2	3	2	3.0%	1
Foeniculum vulgare	sweet fennel	L	8	2	109	28	42.4%	3
Genista monspessulana	**French broom**	L	10	2	70	27	40.9%	**3**
Hedera canariensis	**Algerian ivy**	M	6	2	0	0	0.0%	**3.1**
Hedera helix	English ivy	M	6	2	20	9	13.6%	2
Helichrysum petiolare	**licorice plant**	M	4	2	10	6	9.1%	**1**
Hirschfeldia incana	shortpod mustard		5	2	14	11	16.7%	2
Holcus lanatus	velvet grass, Yorkshire fog	L	7	2	17	10	15.2%	2
Ilex aquifolium	**English holly**	M	5	2	6	3	4.5%	**1**
Leucanthemum vulgare	ox-eye daisy		4	2	19	7	10.6%	2
Mesembryanthemum crystallinum	**ice plant**		5	2	0	0	0.0%	**5**
Nicotiana glauca	tree tobacco		5	2	0	0	0.0%	**3.1**
Oxalis pes-caprae	Bermuda buttercup	M	6	2	6	5	7.6%	2
Phalaris arundinacea	reed canary grass		5	2	2	2	3.0%	**3.1**
Pinus radiata	**Monterey pine**	L	6	2	46	15	22.7%	**3**
Robinia pseudoacacia	**black locust**		5	2	0	0	0.0%	**3.1**
Rumex acetosella	**sheep sorrel**	L	5	2	17	10	15.2%	**3**
Acacia decurrens	**green wattle**	H	3	3				**4**
Albizia lophantha		H	2	3				**3.1**
Aptenia cordifolia	**heartleaf iceplant**	H	3.25	3				**5**
Berberis darwinii	**Darwin's berberis**	H	2	3				**3.1**
Brachypodium distachyon	**purple false brome**		6	3				**3.1**
Brassica rapa	**field mustard**	L	4	3				3
Briza maxima	**big quakinggrass**		4	3				3
Bromus diandrus	**ripgut brome**		5	3				**3.2**
Bromus hordeaceus	**soft brome**		4	3				**4**
Bromus madritensis ssp. *rubens*	**red brome**		7	3				**3.2**
Bromus tectorum	**cheat grass, downy brome**		7	3				**3.2**
Conicosia pugioniformis	**narrow-leaved iceplant**	H	3	3				**5**
Cotoneaster franchetii	orange cotoneaster	L	4	3		13	19.7%	3
Crataegus monogyna	**singleseed hawthorn**	H	2	3				**3.1**
Dactylis glomerata	**orchard grass**	M	5	3				**3.2**
Duchesnea indica	**mock-strawberry**	H	2	3				**4**

10

Table 1. Number of occurrences and species list revisions for GOGA based largely on 2006-2007 field results. Percentages based on 66 subwatersheds searched. Changes in **bold.** (continued).

Scientific Name	Common Name	06-07 Feas-ability of Control	Invasive-ness Score	06-07 list	06-07 #occ	06-07 #suwa	% suwa found in	08 list
Erechtites glomerata	**Australian fireweed, cutleaf burnweed**	L	4	**3**				**3**
Erechtites minima	**Australian fireweed, coastal burnweed**	L	4	**3**				**3**
Festuca arundinacea	tall fescue	M	7	**3**				**3.2**
Marrubium vulgare	horehound	H	3	**3**				**4**
Mentha spicata var. spicata		H	2	**3**				**4**
Paspalum dilatatum	dallis grass	H	3	**3**				**4**
Pennisetum clandestinum	**Kikuyu grass**	M	6	**3**				**3.2**
Phalaris aquatica	Harding grass	M	8	**3**	38	16	24.2%	**3**
Pittosporum crassifolium	stiffleaf cheesewood	H	2	**3**				**3.1**
Pittosporum undulatum	**Victorian box**	H	3	**3**				**4**
Pyracantha angustifolia	**narrowleaf firethorn**	H	2	**3**				**3.1**
Rosa eglanteria	sweetbriar rose	H	2	**3**				**3.2**
Scabiosa atropurpurea	**mourningbride**	H	3	**3**				**4**
Tamarix chinensis	saltcedar		4	**3**				**3**
Xanthium spinosum	spiny cockleburr		4	**3**				**3**
Acacia baileyana	cootamundra wattle		3	4				4
Acacia dealbata	silver wattle		3	4				4
Acacia longifolia	Sydney golden wattle		3	4				4
Acacia mearnsii	black wattle		3	4				4
Acacia verticillata	prickly Moses	M	3	4				4
Allium triquetrum	threecorner leek	M	1	4				4
Alopecurus pratensis	**meadow foxtail**	L	2	**4**				
Amaryllis belladonna	belladonna lily	H	0	4				4
Anredera cordifolia	Madeira vine		2	4				4
Arrhenatherum elatius	tall oatgrass	M	2	4				4
Barbarea verna	early yellowrocket		2	4				4
Barbarea vulgaris	winter cress		2	4				4
Bellardia trixago	bellardia	L	2	4				4
Brassica nigra	black mustard	L	3	4				4
Briza minor	little quakinggrass		2	4				4
Bromus catharticus	rescue grass		2	4				4
Bromus stamineus	roadside brome		2	4				4
Calendula arvensis	field marigold	H	0	4				4
Centaurea diluta	North African knapweed		3	4				4
Centranthus ruber	red valerian	L	2	4				4
Cestrum aurantiacum	orange jessamine	H	0	4				4

Table 1. Number of occurrences and species list revisions for GOGA based largely on 2006-2007 field results. Percentages based on 66 subwatersheds searched. Changes in **bold**. (continued).

Scientific Name	Common Name	06-07 Feas-ability of Control	Invasive-ness Score	06-07 list	06-07 #occ	06-07 #suwa	% suwa found in	08 list
Coprosma repens	creeping mirrorplant	H	1.5	4				4
Cotula australis	Australian waterbuttons		1	4				4
Cotula coronopifolia	brassbuttons	L	2	4				4
Crocosmia X crocosmiiflora	crocosmia, montbretia	M	3	4				4
Cupressus macrocarpa	Monterey cypress	L	2	4				4
Cytisus multiflorus	white spanishbroom		2	4				4
Daucus carota	Queen Anne's lace, wild carrot	M	2	4				4
Digitaria sanguinalis	crabgrass	M	2	4				4
Dipsacus sativus	Indian teasel		3	4				4
Drosanthemum floribundum	**showy dewflower**		1	4				**5**
Echium candicans	pride of Madeira	L	3	4				4
Echium plantagineum	**salvation jane**	M	2	**4**				**3.1**
Euphorbia peplus	petty spurge		1	4				4
Geranium retrorsum	New Zealand geranium		1	4				4
Gunnera tinctoria	Chilean gunnera	H	0	4				4
Hainardia cylindrica	barbgrass		1	4				
Hypericum calycinum	Aaron's beard		1	4				4
Ipomoea mutabilis	oceanblue morning-glory	L	2	4				4
Kniphofia uvaria	redhot poker	H	0	4				4
Lepidium strictum	upright pepperweed		1.75	4				4
Leptospermum laevigatum	**Australian teatree**	M	2	**4**				**3.2**
Ligustrum ovalifolium	california privet		3	4				4
Linaria vulgaris	butter and eggs		2	4				4
Lobularia maritima	sweet alyssum	H	0	4				4
Lonicera japonica	Japanese honeysuckle		3	4				4
Mentha X piperita	peppermint		2	4				4
Muehlenbeckia complexa	maidenhair vine	H	1	4				4
Myosotis latifolia	broadleaf forget-me-not	L	1	4				4
Nerium oleander	**oleander**		1	**4**				
Parapholis incurva	**curved sicklegrass**		1	**4**				
Parentucellia viscosa	yellow glandweed	H	1	4				4
Phalaris canariensis	annual canarygrass		2	4				4
Phalaris minor	**littleseed canarygrass**		2	**4**				
Phalaris paradoxa	**hood canarygrass**		2	**4**				

12

Table 1. Number of occurrences and species list revisions for GOGA based largely on 2006-2007 field results. Percentages based on 66 subwatersheds searched. Changes in **bold.** (continued).

Scientific Name	Common Name	06-07 Feas- ability of Control	Invasive- ness Score	06-07 list	06-07 #occ	06-07 #suwa	% suwa found in	08 list
Polycarpon tetraphyllum	**fourleaf manyseed**		1	**4**				
Prunus avium	bird cherry		1	4				4
Prunus cerasifera	cherry plum	M	2	4				4
Ranunculus muricatus	spinyfruit buttercup	L	2	4				4
Ranunculus repens	creeping buttercup		3	4				4
Raphanus sativus	wild radish	L	3	4				4
Schinus molle	**pepper tree**		3.75	**4**				3
Senecio elegans	redpurple ragwort		3	4				4
Sinapis arvensis	**charlock**		2	**4**				
Sparaxis tricolor hybrid	Harlequin flower		2	4				4
Tetragonia tetragonioides	New Zealand-spinach	H	0	4				4
Tropaeolum majus	nasturtium	H	0	4				4
Verbascum blattaria	moth mullein		1	4				4
Watsonia borbonica	bugle-lily		2	4				4
Watsonia marginata	fragrant bugle-lily		2	4				4
Watsonia meriana	bulbil bugle-lily	M	3	4				4
Xanthium strumarium	**rough cockleburr**		3	**4**				3
Zantedeschia aethiopica	calla lily	L	3	4				4
Ammophila arenaria	European beachgrass	L	10	5				5
Eichhornia crassipes	water hyacinth	L	5	5				5
Myriophyllum aquaticum	parrot's-feather	H	8	5				5
Spartina alterniflora	Atlantic cordgrass	H	10	5				5
Ammophila breviligulata	**American beachgrass**		5					5
Anthoxanthum odoratum	**sweet vernal grass**		6					3.1
Chrysanthemum segetum	**corndaisy**		0					4
Epipactis helleborine	**broadleaf hellebore**		0					4
Erigeron karvinskianus	**Latin American fleabane**	L	0					4
Lathyrus latifolius	**perennial pea**	H	0					4
Leucanthemum maximum	**Shasta daisy**	H	0					4
Myosotis discolor	**forget-me-not**		0					4
Myriophyllum spicatum	**Eurasian watermilfoil**		7					5
Solanum marginatum	**white-margined nightshade**		3					4
Tanacetum parthenium	feverfew		0					4

13

3.4 Outreach

Education and outreach plays a critical role in the engagement of a network of early detectors. A number of "Weed ID" classes were held for GOGA staff, volunteers, interns, Golden Gate National Parks Conservancy staff, and Point Reyes NS volunteers. In total, five classes were held with 47 individuals in attendance. Additionally, three Geoweed/invasive plant mapping trainings were held with 37 attendees.

Whenever possible, volunteers were trained, on an individual basis, to conduct early detection surveys and map incipient populations of target pest plants. Fifteen volunteers over two years were worked with on a one-on-one basis, contributing 543 hours worth $9795.72. Seven of these volunteers were new to volunteering with the parks.

Web pages were created to provide support to Weed Watcher participants (http://science.nature.nps.gov/im/units/sfan/vital_signs/Invasives/weed_watchers.cfm). Online versions of the "Plant-out-of-Place" cards, a narrative explaining the necessity for invasive plant early detection, and information about how to take part in the Weed Watcher program are featured on the web pages. The potential exists to expand these pages to provide online trainings, maps, data sheets, and links to reporting. Until we can track the number of hits to this page, we will be unable to measure the success of online outreach well. A voluntary form generally submittable online (depending on email system and permissions) registered 11 downloads of ID cards, generally from agency and nonprofit users in California and Oregon.

Further development of the volunteer component of the early detection program at the SFAN parks will undoubtedly result in increasing the potential for new detections along the trail and road corridors of the parks. While drop-in volunteers are limited in their capacity for identifying more than a few new plants to them and thus performing Weed Watcher surveys, encouraging drop-ins is a necessary tool for volunteer recruitment and expanding citizen involvement.

4.0 Discussion

4.1 Collaboration

Early detection is meaningless without rapid assessment and response to invasions. The SFAN I&M Network of parks has many invasive plant management teams that manage incipient and established weed populations. The importance of both collaboration and communication with these management teams is imperative to the success of an early detection program.

At GOGA there are several groups that manage invasive species. The Habitat Restoration Team, under the direction of Maria Alvarez, has worked intimately with the Weed Watcher program, including adopting the data management system GeoWeed to facilitate communication between the programs and participating in early detection surveys during their Invasive Plant Patrol roving hikes. There is potential to augment the existing IPP hikes with Weed Watcher hikes to cover a larger area of GOGA. The Habitat Restoration Team works at sites throughout the park, and are host to a sizeable volunteer program of knowledgeable people who have the capacity to respond to new invasions. Continued participation by the Habitat Restoration Team is critical to any successful early detection program at this park.

The Golden Gate National Parks Conservancy (GGNPC) also houses several weed management programs that have participated in the Weed Watcher program including the Native Plant Nurseries at Muir Woods, the Marin Headlands, and the Presidio. The Site Stewardship restoration programs housed at the GGNPC manage areas in Sweeney Ridge, Mori Point, and Tennessee Valley. These groups also have made commitments to utilize the GeoWeed data management system, which could facilitate communication of findings.

Point Reyes National Seashore has a well-established weed management program with an affiliated volunteer program, the Habitat Restoration Program (HRP). The Weed Watcher program has only begun to work with these programs, hosting a "Weed ID" course and several early detection surveys with resource staff. Additional work is planned for 2008.

Also housed at Point Reyes NS is the California Exotic Plant Management Team (EPMT) which is responsible for managing weed populations at national parks across California. The EPMT program is integral to rapid response at parks that are not served by in-house management programs, or as an augmentation to existing programs.

Some work has been done with the resource staff at Pinnacles National Monument, including demonstrations of GeoWeed and small botanical surveys for incipient populations (see, e.g., Williams, Franket and Speith 2008). Further development of this program should occur in 2008 and 2009.

Further work at other SFAN network parks is necessary to ensure that findings will be communicated to the responsible entities for rapid response. Reliance upon shared data via the GeoWeed system is only one step in a communication process that should include an alert system of emails, reports, and phone calls. This component of the Weed Watcher program needs to be streamlined and formalized, so that responsible entities for each region of network parks can be notified in a timely manner about Weed Watcher findings.

As network parks share borders with many other land management agencies, an integrated approach is key to stopping the spread of new invaders. In addition to working with the network of parks, I&M staff have helped to secure grant funding to build a true Bay Area Early Detection Network (BAEDN) for the nine-county area. An initial partner interest meeting in December 2006 was followed by intermittent conference calls and presentations, and resulted in a coalition of over 50 potentially and actively interested organizations representing national, state and local agencies, nonprofits, and individuals. With funds delivered in 2008, work will begin in earnest and is expected to include online reporting, hiring a coordinator for BAEDN, and trainings based largely on SFAN protocols, so that parks will no longer be limited to seeing only what is within our borders.

6.0 Literature Cited

Golden Gate National Recreation Area. 2004. 2004 rare plant monitoring report. Unpublished report on file at GOGA.

McNeely, J. A., H. A. Mooney, L. E. Neville, P. J. Schei, and J. K. Waage, eds. 2001. Global strategy on invasive alien species. IUCN. Available at: http://www.iucn.org/ (accessed 31 August 2006).

Scott, J.M. and D.S. Wilcove. 1998. Improving the future for endangered species. Bioscience. **48**(8): 579-80.

Williams, A. E., S. Franklet, and E. Speith. 2008. Botanical inventory of Pinnacles National Monument's new lands. Natural Resource Report NPS/PWR/SFAN/NRTR—2008/083. National Park Service, Oakland, California.

Williams, A. E, S. O'Neil, E. Speith, and J. Rodgers. 2008 (in review). Early detection monitoring of invasive plant species in the San Francisco Bay Area Network: A volunteer-based approach. Natural Resource Report NPS/PWR/SFAN/NRR—2008/00N. National Park Service, Oakland, California.

7.0 Glossary

Assessments: Surveys and monitoring of isolated weeds and weed population *occurrences* are defined and recorded in the database as individual *assessments*. An *assessment* therefore is a set of measurements taken over time, recorded for a specified weed *occurrence*. Each *assessment* relates to one specific *occurrence*, while each *occurrence* can accrue a series of *assessments* over time. An *assessment* for each *occurrence* can be recorded as a point, a line, or a polygon. *Assessments* will be used to depict the size, scale, and coverage of an occurrence and therefore will be used as a basis for monitoring the project's effectiveness. The initial *occurrence* and *assessment* data will serve as the baseline for the entire project area, and the project area will be re-assessed annually for the duration of the project. These periodic *assessments* will be used to determine if weed populations are increasing or decreasing in size and distribution and if *treatments* are having the desired effects.

Exotic: Occurring in a given place as a result of direct or indirect, deliberate or accidental actions by humans. Synonyms: alien, introduced, non-native, and non-indigenous.

GeoWeed: The Microsoft Access-based database developed by the Sonoma Ecology Center from the Weed Information Management System. GeoWeed is a relational database that offers digital data collection of management and spatial weed data through ESRI ArcPad applets. The San Francisco Bay Area Network uses GeoWeed for its Early Detection data. Additional information available in SFAN's protocol and at http://geoweed.org.

Invasive: Tending to spread, intrude, or encroach, usually aggressively and in a hurtful manner. Gardeners characterize cultivated plants as "invasive" when they spread aggressively beyond where they were intended to remain, particularly if they outcompete and displace other plants in the garden. Native species can behave invasively, but this term generally connotes non-natives which can spread into undisturbed ecosystems.

Invasive species: Official term for an exotic species whose introduction can cause economic or environmental harm or harm to human health. The term originated in Presidential Executive Order 13112 issued February 3, 1999.

IPP: Invasive Plant Patrol. Early detection program implemented at Golden Gate National Recreation Area.

Management units: Areas to be monitored for new species/infestations. A management unit may be the entire park, critical habitat within a park, or areas of concern given their proximity to known entry points. Some parks define areas by watershed, others use site names–both are considered a management unit.

Occurrences: The weed *occurrence* is the basic unit of mapping and assessing a singular weed or weed population/infestation within WIMS and GeoWeed. Each *occurrence* defines the presence of a single species and is recorded at a specific location. The *occurrence* location is recorded as a point in space, although each *occurrence* may actually be a population of plants covering an extensive area.

Regions: A region is a uniquely named parcel of land that may have either legally defined boundaries or locally derived place names. In the protocol we may use up to three *regions* to locate each *occurrence;* one is mandatory: the sub-watershed (*e.g.* Fort Mason is in GGNRA26-3). *Regions* are synonymous with *area* in WIMS.

SOP: Standard Operating Procedures. These are the detailed steps explaining how to carry out the monitoring protocol.

Subwatershed: A management unit subunit of a watershed, based largely on drainages, and used to track weed work in GOGA.

Survey area: A point with typed-in length and width data, the *survey area* is mapped and documented each survey as a way of showing what area was surveyed, thus showing where target species were NOT found. The *survey area* tab in GeoWeed allows collection of negative data (species name with 0% cover and no phenology information), as well as a full inventory of plants seen (species name, % cover, phenology, identification confidence and reason for doubt). The *survey area* point is augmented by a tracklog for more detailed visualization of the survey route.

Treatments: A *treatment* is any weed management activity that occurs at a specific time over a defined geographical area. One *treatment* may affect one or more *occurrences* (of one or several species) over one or more *regions*. The WIMS and GeoWeed databases track all types of weed control methods, including manual and mechanical methods, prescribed fire, grazing, biological control, and any chemical treatments. The database also keeps track of how much staff and/or volunteer time has been spent controlling weeds.

Weed: A weed is a plant out of place. This term is subjective; a weed is not necessarily an exotic species, although the terms are growing more synonymous. The term "noxious weed" is an official designation for weeds which cause major economic harm. Plants introduced for their ornamental, utilitarian, or food value which "escape" and disrupt natural ecosystems have only recently been recognized as weeds. More precise, accepted, and general terms for environmentally harmful non-natives are exotic pest plant (although "pest" has a legal definition of causing harm, similar to "noxious") and invasive plant species. In Australia, exotic pest plants are termed environmental weeds.

Appendix A. Maps showing prioritized subwatersheds.

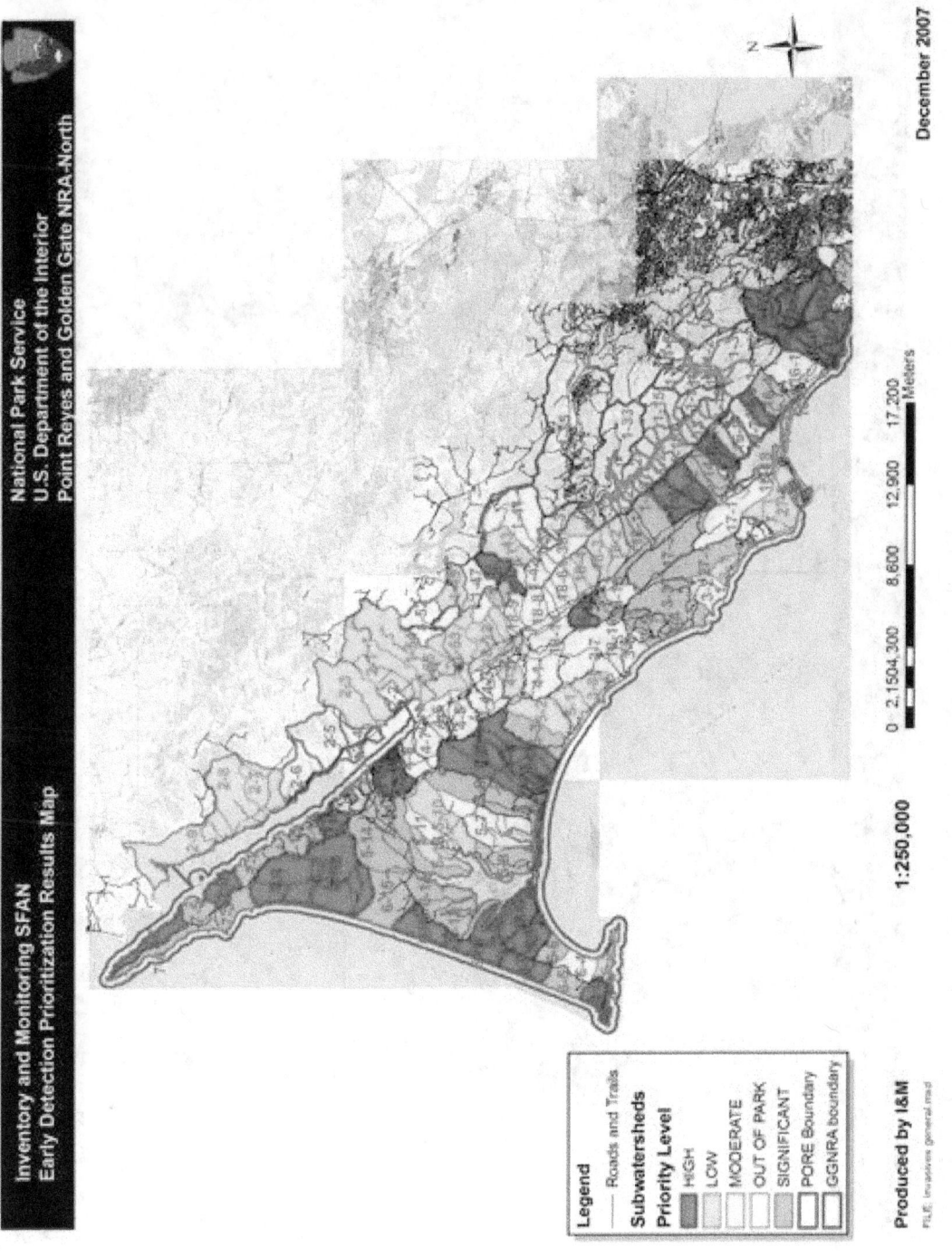

Inventory and Monitoring SFAN
Early Detection Prioritization Results Map

National Park Service
U.S. Department of the Interior
Point Reyes and Golden Gate NRA-North

Legend

Roads and Trails

Subwatersheds
Priority Level

HIGH
LOW
MODERATE
OUT OF PARK
SIGNIFICANT
PORE Boundary
GGNRA boundary

Produced by I&M

1:250,000

0 2,1504,300   8,600   12,900   17,200
                                    Meters

December 2007

21

Appendix A. Maps showing prioritized subwatersheds. (continued)

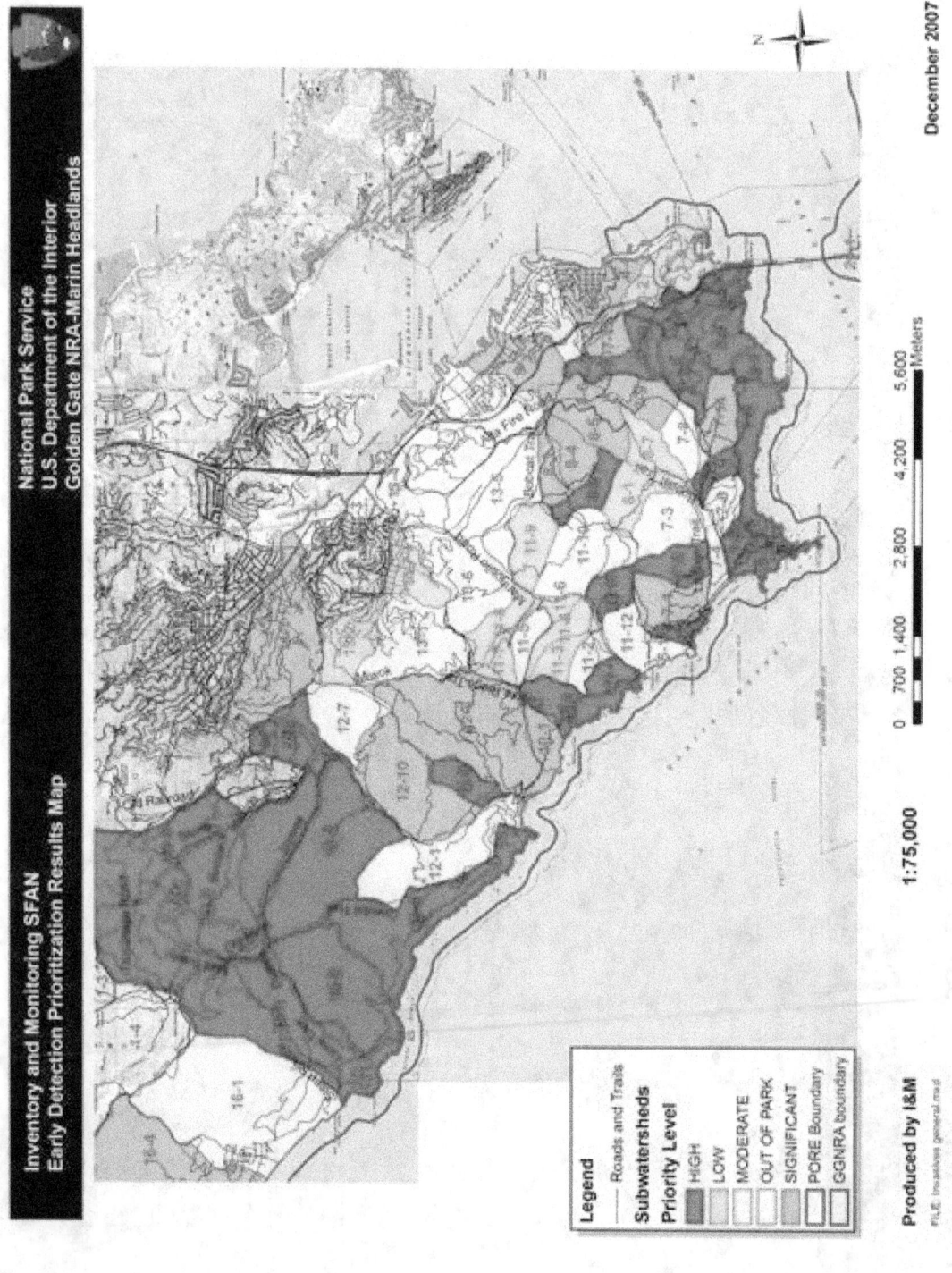

Inventory and Monitoring SFAN
Early Detection Prioritization Results Map

National Park Service
U.S. Department of the Interior
Golden Gate NRA-Marin Headlands

Legend
Roads and Trails
Subwatersheds
Priority Level
HIGH
LOW
MODERATE
OUT OF PARK
SIGNIFICANT
PORE Boundary
GGNRA boundary

1:75,000

0 700 1,400   2,800   4,200   5,600
                                          Meters

Produced by I&M

December 2007

22

Appendix A. Maps showing prioritized subwatersheds. (continued)

Inventory and Monitoring SFAN
Early Detection Prioritization Results Map

National Park Service
U.S. Department of the Interior
Golden Gate NRA-Presidio and South

Legend
☐ GGNRA boundary
Subwatersheds
Priority Level
■ HIGH
☐ LOW
☐ MODERATE
☐ OUT OF PARK
☐ SIGNIFICANT

Produced by I&M
FILE: Invasives general map

1:175,000

0   1,750 3,500   7,000   10,500   14,000
                                    Meters

December 2007

Appendix B: List of priority invasive species by park (2007).
Golden Gate, Muir Woods, Presidio and Fort Point: Priority 1 Species
Point occurrences and polygon assessments

Scientific Name	Common Name	Family	PLANTS Code
Ailanthus altissima	tree-of-heaven	Simaroubaceae	AIAL
Arctotheca calendula	capeweed	Asteraceae	ARCA45
Arundo donax	giant reed	Poaceae	ARDO4
Carduus acanthoides	plumeless thistle	Asteraceae	CAAC
Carthamus lanatus	woolly distaff thistle	Asteraceae	CALA20
Centaurea calcitrapa	purple starthistle	Asteraceae	CECA2
Centaurea solstitialis	yellow starthistle	Asteraceae	CESO3
Cirsium arvense	Canada thistle	Asteraceae	CIAR4
Cortaderia jubata	Andean or purple pampas grass, jubata grass	Poaceae	COJU2
Cortaderia selloana	Uruguayan pampas grass	Poaceae	COSE4
Cotoneaster pannosus	silverleaf cotoneaster	Rosaceae	COPA14
Cynodon dactylon	Bermudagrass	Poaceae	CYDA
Cytisus striatus	Portugese broom, striated broom	Fabaceae	CYST7
Digitalis purpurea	purple foxglove	Scrophulariaceae	DIPU
Dittrichia graveolens	stinkweed	Asteraceae	DIGR4
Ehrharta calycina	perennial veldt grass	Poaceae	EHCA
Ehrharta erecta	panic veldt grass	Poaceae	EHER
Hypericum perforatum	Klamathweed	Clusiaceae	HYPE
Mentha pulegium	pennyroyal	Lamiaceae	MEPU
Rubus discolor [*procerus, armeniacus*]	Himalayan blackberry	Rosaceae	RUDI2
Spartium junceum	Spanish broom	Fabaceae	SPJU2
Ulex europaea	gorse, furze	Fabaceae	ULEU
Vinca major	periwinkle	Apocynaceae	VIMA

Appendix B: List of priority invasive species by park (2007) (continued).
Golden Gate, Muir Woods, Presidio and Fort Point: Priority 2 Species
Point occurrences and polygon assessments (if patch size <100m^2)

Scientific Name	Common Name	Family	PLANTS Code
Acacia melanoxylon	blackwood acacia	Fabaceae	ACME
Ageratina adenophora	thoroughwort, crofton weed	Asteraceae	AGAD2
Carduus tenuiflorus	slender-flowered thistle	Asteraceae	CATE2
Carpobrotus chilensis	sea fig	Aizoaceae	CACH38
Carpobrotus edulis	hottentot fig, freeway iceplant	Aizoaceae	CAED3
Centaurea melitensis	Napa thistle, tocalote	Asteraceae	CEME2
Conium maculatum	poison hemlock	Apiaceae	COMA2
Cynara cardunculus	artichoke thistle, cardoon	Asteraceae	CYCA
Cytisus scoparius	Scotch broom	Fabaceae	CYSC4
Delairea odorata	cape ivy	Asteraceae	DEOD
Dipsacus fullonum	common teasel, Fuller's teasel	Dipsacaceae	DIFU2
Eucalyptus globulus	bluegum eucalyptus	Myrtaceae	EUGL
Euphorbia oblongata	eggleaf or oblong spurge	Euphorbiaceae	EUOB4
Foeniculum vulgare	sweet fennel	Apiaceae	FOVU
Genista monspessulana	French broom	Fabaceae	GEMO2
Hedera canariensis	Algerian ivy	Araliaceae	HEDCA
Hedera helix	English ivy	Araliaceae	HEHE
Helichrysum petiolare	licorice plant	Asteraceae	HEPE8
Hirschfeldia incana	shortpod mustard	Brassicaceae	HIIN3
Holcus lanatus	velvet grass, Yorkshire fog	Poaceae	HOLA
Ilex aquifolium	English holly	Aquifoliaceae	ILAQ80
Leucanthemum vulgare	ox-eye daisy	Asteraceae	LEVU
Mesembryanthemum crystallinum	crystalline ice plant	Aizoaceae	MECR3
Nicotiana glauca	tree tobacco	Solanaceae	NIGL
Oxalis pes-caprae	Bermuda buttercup	Oxalidaceae	OXPE
Phalaris arundinacea	reed canary grass	Poaceae	PHAR3
Pinus radiata	Monterey pine	Pinaceae	PIRA2
Robinia pseudoacacia	black locust	Fabaceae	ROPS
Rumex acetosella	sheep sorrel	Polygonaceae	RUAC3

Golden Gate, Muir Woods, Presidio and Fort Point: Priority 3 Species
Presence/absence, or point occurrences (if patch size <100m^2)

Scientific Name	Common Name	Family	PLANTS Code
Acacia decurrens	green wattle	Fabaceae	ACDE
Albizia lophantha	silk tree; cape wattle	Fabaceae	ALLO
Aptenia cordifolia	heartleaf iceplant	Aizoaceae	APCO
Berberis darwinii	Darwin's berberis	Berberidaceae	BEDA
Brachypodium distachyon	purple false brome	Poaceae	BRDI2
Brassica rapa	field mustard	Brassicaceae	BRRA
Briza maxima	big quakinggrass	Poaceae	BRMA
Bromus diandrus	ripgut brome	Poaceae	BRDI3
Bromus hordeaceus	soft brome	Poaceae	BRHO2
Bromus madritensis ssp. *rubens*	red brome	Poaceae	BRMAR
Bromus tectorum	cheat grass, downy brome	Poaceae	BRTE
Conicosia pugioniformis	narrow-leaved iceplant	Aizoaceae	COPU18
Cotoneaster franchetii	orange cotoneaster	Rosaceae	COFR3
Crataegus monogyna	singleseed hawthorn	Rosaceae	CRMO
Dactylis glomerata	orchard grass, cocksfoot	Poaceae	DAGL
Duchesnea indica	mock-strawberry	Rosaceae	DUIN
Erechtites glomerata	Australian fireweed, cutleaf burnweed	Asteraceae	ERGL8
Erechtites minima	Australian fireweed, coastal burnweed	Asteraceae	ERMI6
Festuca arundinacea	tall fescue	Poaceae	FEAR3
Marrubium vulgare	horehound	Lamiaceae	MAVU
Mentha spicata var. *spicata*	spearmint	Lamiaceae	MESP3
Paspalum dilatatum	dallis grass	Poaceae	PADI3
Pennisetum clandestinum	Kikuyu grass	Poaceae	PECL2
Phalaris aquatica	Harding grass	Poaceae	PHAQ
Pittosporum crassifolium	stiffleaf cheesewood	Pittosporaceae	PICR
Pittosporum undulatum	Victorian box	Pittosporaceae	PIUN2
Pyracantha angustifolia	narrowleaf firethorn	Rosaceae	PYAN
Rosa eglanteria	sweetbriar rose	Rosaceae	ROEG
Scabiosa atropurpurea	mourningbride	Dipsacaceae	SCAT
Tamarix chinensis	saltcedar	Tamaricaceae	TACH2
Xanthium spinosum	spiny cockleburr	Asteraceae	XASP2

Golden Gate, Muir Woods, Presidio and Fort Point: Priority 4 Species

Presence/absence (advanced observers)

Scientific Name	Common Name	Family	PLANTS Code
Acacia baileyana	cootamundra wattle	Fabaceae	ACBA
Acacia dealbata	silver wattle	Fabaceae	ACDE3
Acacia longifolia	Sydney golden wattle	Fabaceae	ACLO
Acacia mearnsii	black wattle	Fabaceae	ACME80
Acacia verticillata	prickly Moses	Fabaceae	ACVE2
Allium triquetrum	threecorner leek	Liliaceae	ALTR4
Alopecurus pratensis	meadow foxtail	Poaceae	ALPR3
Amaryllis belladonna	belladonna lily	Liliaceae	AMBE3
Anredera cordifolia	Madeira vine	Basellaceae	ANCO6
Arrhenatherum elatius	tall oatgrass	Poaceae	AREL3
Barbarea verna	early yellowrocket	Brassicaceae	BAVE
Barbarea vulgaris	winter cress	Brassicaceae	BAVU
Bellardia trixago	bellardia	Scrophulariaceae	BETR
Brassica nigra	black mustard	Brassicaceae	BRNI
Briza minor	little quakinggrass	Poaceae	BRMI2
Bromus catharticus	rescue grass	Poaceae	BRCA6
Bromus stamineus	roadside brome	Poaceae	BRST3
Calendula arvensis	field marigold	Asteraceae	CAAR
Centaurea diluta	North African knapweed	Asteraceae	CEDI4
Centranthus ruber	red valerian	Valerianaceae	CERU2
Cestrum aurantiacum	orange jessamine	Solanaceae	CEAU2
Coprosma repens	creeping mirrorplant	Rubiaceae	CORE4
Cotula australis	Australian waterbuttons	Asteraceae	COAU3
Cotula coronopifolia	brassbuttons	Asteraceae	COCO7
Crocosmia X crocosmiiflora	crocosmia, montbretia	Iridaceae	CRCR6
Cupressus macrocarpa	Monterey cypress	Cupressaceae	CUMA2
Cytisus multiflorus	white spanishbroom	Fabaceae	CYMU3
Daucus carota	Queen Anne's lace, wild carrot	Apiaceae	DACA6
Digitaria sanguinalis	crabgrass	Poaceae	DISA
Dipsacus sativus	Indian teasel	Dipsacaceae	DISA9
Drosanthemum floribundum	showy dewflower	Aizoaceae	DRFL2
Echium candicans	pride of Madeira	Boraginaceae	ECCA5
Echium plantagineum	salvation jane	Boraginaceae	ECPL
Euphorbia peplus	petty spurge	Euphorbiaceae	EUPE6
Geranium retrorsum	New Zealand geranium	Geraniaceae	GERE
Gunnera tinctoria	Chilean gunnera	Gunneraceae	GUTI
Hainardia cylindrica	barbgrass	Poaceae	HACY
Hypericum calycinum	Aaron's beard	Clusiaceae	HYCA10
Ipomoea mutabilis	oceanblue morning-glory	Convolvulaceae	IPMU6
Kniphofia uvaria	redhot poker	Liliaceae	KNUV80

Appendix B: List of priority invasive species by park (2007) (continued).
Priority 4 Species, continued

Scientific Name	Common Name	Family	PLANTS Code
Lepidium strictum	upright pepperweed	Brassicaceae	LEST2
Leptospermum laevigatum	Australian teatree	Myrtaceae	LELA29
Ligustrum ovalifolium	california privet	Oleaceae	LIOV
Linaria vulgaris	butter and eggs	Scrophulariaceae	LIVU2
Lobularia maritima	sweet alyssum	Brassicaceae	LOMA
Lonicera japonica	Japanese honeysuckle	Caprifoliaceae	LOJA
Mentha X piperita	peppermint	Lamiaceae	MEPI
Muehlenbeckia complexa	maidenhair vine	Polygonaceae	MUCO3
Myosotis latifolia	broadleaf forget-me-not	Boraginaceae	MYLA4
Nerium oleander	oleander	Apocynaceae	NEOL
Parapholis incurva	curved sicklegrass	Poaceae	PAIN
Parentucellia viscosa	yellow glandweed	Scrophulariaceae	PAVI3
Phalaris canariensis	annual canarygrass	Poaceae	PHCA5
Phalaris minor	littleseed canarygrass	Poaceae	PHMI3
Phalaris paradoxa	hood canarygrass	Poaceae	PHPA5
Polycarpon tetraphyllum	fourleaf manyseed	Caryophyllaceae	POTE
Prunus avium	bird cherry	Rosaceae	PRAV
Prunus cerasifera	cherry plum	Rosaceae	PRCE2
Ranunculus muricatus	spinyfruit buttercup	Ranunculaceae	RAMU2
Ranunculus repens	creeping buttercup	Ranunculaceae	RARE3
Raphanus sativus	wild radish	Brassicaceae	RASA2
Schinus molle	pepper tree	Anacardiaceae	SCMO
Senecio elegans	redpurple ragwort	Asteraceae	SEEL
Sinapis arvensis	charlock	Brassicaceae	SIAR4
Sparaxis tricolor hybrid	Harlequin flower	Iridaceae	SPTR
Tetragonia tetragonioides	New Zealand-spinach	Aizoaceae	TETE3
Tropaeolum majus	nasturtium	Tropaeolaceae	TRMA7
Verbascum blattaria	moth mullein	Scrophulariaceae	VEBL
Watsonia borbonica	bugle-lily	Iridaceae	WABO
Watsonia marginata	fragrant bugle-lily	Iridaceae	WAMA2
Watsonia meriana	bulbil bugle-lily	Iridaceae	WAME
Xanthium strumarium	rough cockleburr	Asteraceae	XAST
Zantedeschia aethiopica	calla lily	Araceae	ZAAE

Golden Gate, Muir Woods, Presidio and Fort Point: Priority 5 Species

(Dune and Aquatic)

Scientific Name	Common Name	Family	PLANTS Code
Ammophila arenaria	European beachgrass	Poaceae	AMAR4
Eichhornia crassipes	water hyacinth	Pontederiaceae	EICR
Spartina alterniflora	Atlantic or smooth cordgrass	Poaceae	SPAL

Appendix C. Maps showing survey results.

Available online at
http://science.nature.nps.gov/im/units/sfan/vital_signs/Invasives/report_maps.cfm

NPS D-44, November 2008

www.ingramcontent.com/pod-product-compliance
Lightning Source LLC
Chambersburg PA
CBHW080922290526
45795CB00007BA/2623